The Emperor's Clothes Cost Twenty Dollars

The book is about the difference between Federal Reserve Notes and honest money

by Lloyd Darland

First Edition—First Printing, August, 1977
Second Edition (Revised)—First Printing, October, 1980
Second Edition—Second Printing, February, 1981
Third Edition—June, 2011
Original Artwork by Steve Klein

The information contained in this book is meant to educate the reader, and is in no way intended to provide medical, financial, legal or any other services for individual problems or circumstances. We encourage readers to seek advice from competent professionals for personal health, financial and legal needs.

This information is published under the First Amendment of the Constitution of the United States, which guarantees the right to discuss openly and freely all matters of public concern and to express viewpoints, no matter how controversial or unaccepted they may be. Any references for additional information that we may provide are for the reader's benefit only and are not affiliated with *The Bob Livingston Letter*™ in any way, unless otherwise stated. All information is believed to be correct, but its accuracy cannot be guaranteed. The owner, publisher and editor are not responsible for errors and omissions.

Published by *The Bob Livingston Letter*™
P.O. Box 1105, Cullman, AL 35056

www.BobLivingstonLetter.com
www.PersonalLiberty.com

The Emperor's Clothes Cost Twenty Dollars

Contents

Foreword

You've probably heard the story—or at least some of it. About how, in the dead of night in 1913, a group of United States lawmakers met with top executives from the world's biggest banks and corporations on a remote island off the coast of Georgia and laid the groundwork for a central bank.

About how those lawmakers and President Woodrow Wilson conspired to deceive the American people, using a banking crisis created by the big banksters as a backdrop, to sell them on the need for a central bank. About how some of those same lawmakers lied and used doublespeak to convince Americans they were against the very law they were writing in order to trick Americans into believing the bill would be beneficial and ensure its passage.

And you've no doubt heard—especially lately—how the Federal Reserve, the central bank created out of that meeting so long ago, is directly responsible for the economic situation we now find ourselves in. You've heard it, but maybe you didn't believe it. Or maybe you didn't understand it.

That's because most of the books that describe the Federal Reserve System and the inflation it created are not easy reads. Face it; reading about finance and inflation can be boring. Many people these days find little time for reading at all, especially about something that happened so long ago and seems so complicated.

You may have wanted to learn more, but you were looking for a faster, easier way to learn it. You wanted something that, once you read it, you slapped your forehead and said, "Aha. Now I understand."

That's what makes *The Emperor's Clothes Cost Twenty Dollars* such a fascinating book... and why we've acquired the rights to reprint it—even though it was first printed more than 30 years ago.

The book's author, Lloyd Darland, first learned about finance as a young boy in Depression-era America. He says he had his heart set on buying a balsa wood glider. They could be bought for 5 cents each, or two for a dime. Although his parents dissuaded him and said the plane was a waste of money, Darland wanted it so badly that he saved, scrimped and cajoled his parents out of a second nickel so he would have the 10 cents to buy two planes.

Later, as Darland relates in this book, he experienced the effects of inflation first-hand. He had saved enough money to buy a car he wanted, but his father talked him into investing the money rather than spending it. Ten years later, that money had gained interest, but because of inflation, it would no longer buy a car of similar value.

He wanted to know what happened to his money. Why would his money, which had increased by more than 33 percent in 10 years, not buy as much vehicle as it would before? This perplexed him, so he began to study economics.

He learned his economics lessons so well that he later taught basic economics to first-year college students. The experience opened his eyes. He learned that students—all of whom were high school graduates or held high school equivalency certificates—knew little to nothing about money and how it worked. It was while teaching these classes that the idea to write *The Emperor's Clothes* came to him—sparked by encouragement from a student who asked Darland: "Does anybody else know this stuff?"

Darland realized that maybe too few people did know it, and what better way was there to communicate ideas in the 1970s than to write a book? So he did.

Now you're thinking: "This book was written in the 70s? What possible relevance could a book that is more than 30 years old have to today's circumstances?"

Well, that's the beauty of *The Emperor's Clothes*. It is a timeless tome, and it has the added benefit of being even more relevant today than it was 30 years ago. That's because the circumstances Darland wrote about are playing themselves out today, exactly as he described.

In *The Emperor's Clothes*, Darland explains how the Federal Reserve works to steal your money through inflation, and he describes the fraud and illegalities of the Federal tax system. He uses easy-to-understand analogies, simple language and a little bit of history to make his case that the U.S. government has committed what he calls megafraud on the American people.

Darland thought *The Emperor's Clothes* would make a splash. "I thought people would go crazy over it," he says. In fact it did make a splash... in the halls of power in Washington, D.C. Less than 100 hours after his book hit the streets, the U.S. Secret Service was calling him. What caught the Secret Service's attention was Darland's description of his own honest, private currency in Chapter 4.

For a while, Darland issued currency backed by gold and redeemable in gold coin. The Secret Service "invited" him to Baltimore for a meeting and suggested he bring an attorney when he came. During their meeting with a

Secret Service agent, Darland's attorney asked the agent what law he thought Darland had violated. "You can't counterfeit currency," the agent replied. Darland's attorney pointed out that his currency could not be considered counterfeit since it looked nothing like a Federal Reserve Note. After becoming satisfied that what Darland was doing couldn't be considered counterfeiting, the agent told Darland he couldn't make currency for less than $1. Darland had an answer for that. His currency was worth $20. Baffled, the agent told Darland, "I'll be in touch." He never heard from them again on the matter. However, he was now on their radar.

Years later, Darland began a business filling out tax returns. After several years, the Federal government came down on him and charged him with not complying with tax law, even though during the trial an Internal Revenue Service employee testified that the IRS had reviewed more than 600 returns Darland had filed for people and had not found a single mistake.

He was eventually convicted of failing to pay the proper taxes for his tax business and spent 21 months in Federal prison.

Of course, it's the Federal government that is the criminal enterprise. It has been stealing the wealth of Americans through the unConstitutional Federal Reserve since 1914. But the system is rigged. The tax-payer gets his pocket picked, and no one is the wiser.

Once you read through *The Emperor's Clothes Cost Twenty Dollars*, you'll understand this better than ever.

I mentioned earlier that *The Emperor's Clothes* was timeless. Actually, that's not entirely correct. What it is, despite being first published in 1977, is incredibly TIMELY. You'll be amazed at how the events Darland wrote about in the late 70s and early 80s—the last printing of this book occurred in 1981—continue to play themselves out today. Only they are much, much worse. And even more amazing are the uncanny predictions Darland made then that are coming true now.

So you can see the magnitude of the megafraud government has foisted upon us, we're reprinting the book as it appeared in 1981—virtually unedited, save for some changes for style and grammar. So when you see the price of a house or an ounce of gold or a gallon of gas or something else mentioned that you know is no longer valid, those can serve to drive home Darland's point: that the Federal Reserve system is stealing your wealth.

Best wishes,
Bob Livingston

Preface

John Maynard Keynes once said the surest way to destroy a society is to debauch its currency in such a way that not one person in a million is able to figure out what happened. This book is an attempt to change the odds.

Certainly, I am not the first to wonder what is going on. I have read several excellent books on the currency situation. But the real question is what to do about it. In this book I try to explain the situation in a way that anyone interested should understand and yet be as technically precise as possible so it can withstand close analysis. I lay no claim to being a professional writer. Brevity has required that points which could be greatly expanded are scarcely touched. At other places there are digressions from the main theme to round out an idea.

Though I am grateful for the professional legal, economic and other assistance given, I accept responsibility for the story I have presented. But it is more than a story; it is a book of action.

—Lloyd Darland

Dedication

This is dedicated to my mother and father who must have had a very exciting time with such an active child, and to my grandchildren and others not yet even conceived, as representative of the future of our Country.

About the Author

One hundred and seventy years after the founding of our Country, Mr. Darland entered West Point, where the motto of "Duty, Honor, Country" was more than just three words on an emblem. Though he graduated in the top third of his class, he was more a man of action than of contemplation. Married on graduation day, he and his wife, Lois raised a family of four children.

His work as a youth caused him to be a union member—first in the construction trades and later as a meat cutter. While in the Armed Forces, he became an expert in weapons and explosives. As a project officer working with nuclear weapons he had TOP SECRET clearance. He was a quality control engineer for the Air Force and an operations research analyst for the Army, specializing in cost and economic analysis in the logistics section of an analysis agency. After he retired he became self-employed.

But there is more to life than work. He was a Sunday school teacher in the Methodist Church where he was a member. He designed and built a major addition on his home. He got his pilot's license. He did significant volunteer work in the Maryland prison system, organizing and teaching the first economics class ever presented within the penitentiary walls. He served on the board of directors of the Harford County Gifted and Talented Association, and a a lecturer in economics at the Harford Community College.

He was a firm believer in the ideals that made this Country great and was dedicated to freedom, personal responsibility and the free enterprise system.

Mr. Darland passed away suddenly on August 8, 2011, while we were working to reprint his book.

What's Going On?

Today, just like yesterday, and possibly tomorrow, a thief sneaks into your home, into your wallet, and takes $5. No, this isn't the income tax; that's bad enough, but this is in addition to that. And not just your home; it's happening in every home in the country, every day of the year. This is the average amount taken every day with this quiet method. This book tells how it's done and why, what it means and what you can do about it. The villain is not big business, labor unions, free enter-

prise or local government. The thief is your Federal government! They have incubated a special cancer—the same kind that killed Imperial Rome—and have spread it through the land. The Founders of our Country thought they had written the Constitution to shield us from this disease, but this defense has been penetrated. This book is a call to arms to repair our defenses, lest the thief steal our entire country. The process is inadequately called "inflation." It's really an illness. Whether or not the thievery continues until the destruction is complete depends on what actions are taken. You can help stop it.

Our national money system is sick with this cancer that is gobbling up our dollars and everything measured by them. This cancer has been growing for more than 30 years. It affects and threatens everyone, particularly those who have retired, those who expect to retire, or those who are saving for the future. This cancer is called "inflation," and it's time to do something about it. For years, I was taught that the disease was accidental, but now I find it had been planned. Please read this entire text with an open mind so that you can see through the fog that has been puffed up to confuse us. Some skeptics may try to deceive you by twisting my statements and quoting them out of context, but I honestly try to answer the questions I think you might have. I address this to all concerned citizens who are interested in our Country's survival, and their own.

My interest in this began early. When I was a teenager I earned about $1,500, which would buy a big Buick. My father urged me not to spend the cash on a car but to invest it. I bought war bonds; and in 10 years, my $1,500 had grown to $2,000. But the $2,000 wouldn't buy an average Ford. I felt cheated. The numbers were bigger, but the value was smaller. Something had been taken from me. I decided to see if I could find out who took it and how it was done and decide if anything could be done about it. That's where this project got started. I found out that I had been intentionally cheated, that it had been done with dishonest money and the one in charge of the money was the government. Now, I'm seeing what can be done about it.

I believe that "we the people," under our Constitution, have a right to an honest money system. We do not have it now. I have discovered a way honest money can be brought about with a minimum of delay. The way is startling in its simplicity: to strictly abide by the Constitution. The success of this action in helping to correct the dishonesty in our nation's money structure will greatly benefit everyone who works for a living, everyone who is self-employed and small business owners. It will benefit those who are trying to save a "buck," the retired and those poor souls living on a fixed income. An honest money system would dramatically reduce taxes and at the same time increase the effectiveness of government. I will not try to list every possible benefit, and I suspect that some politicians, as we shall see, will not be happy with sound money. Those who have been living off the phony-money fraud might even be encouraged to get an honest job. Others might say, "Are we not our brother's keeper?" I would respond by saying that each must decide for himself. But in any case, it is not my brother's position to make the decision that I must keep him. I cannot decide for you. I do not want you to decide for me.

To establish a better framework to understand what I am doing, it is best to have some understanding of economics. A simplified model would be to consider that we're all playing in a big game similar to Monopoly®.[1] All the players turn in pennies to get $100 bills in play money. In this game you may trade your time to someone else who wants it, and for this you get some more pay in play money. You use your play money to trade with someone else who has something that you would like to have. If you would prefer, you may make something that others would like to have and trade it to them for some of their play money. The overriding rules of our game will be the Constitution. Under it, you decide who is going to be the head administrator of the rules, and he's called President. You decide who's going to work out what the rules should be, and that group is called the Legislature. You have some people to keep the scraps between players under control, and that group is called the Police. In case there are disagreements between players that the police can't resolve, you have another group, and they are called the Courts. You put someone in charge of making sure that no outside bullies break up your game; they are called "defense." In order to pay for the structure, you set up a system so that there's a "cut" taken each time you do something for someone else, and that's called an "income tax." You set up rules that the makers of things have to comply with, and the expense of these rules have to be included in their price, so those taxes are "hidden." Anytime the players want, they can turn in their play money and get a penny back for each $100 bill. Thus, the stage is set.

Let's make you President

One of the first things you, as President, notice is that the people who don't have anything to sell or don't do anything don't have any money. That doesn't seem fair because, after all, everyone wants to play. Since everyone has a say in who is to be in the various positions, including yours, you want everyone to be as happy as possible. You ask the people who have some cash and who are earning more to give you some extra so that you can give some to the people who don't have any. Sure enough they do. But pretty soon the people you have given money to have spent it and are again without any. So you ask for an increase in the income tax so you can give even more to the others. But then a couple of things happen. First, there was someone who was working, but he didn't have very much and he saw that you were giving people who didn't work as much money as he was making. He quickly figured out that if he wasn't working, then he would be better off. He quit working, and sure enough he was better off. Further, the people who were making more than that noticed that what they had left wouldn't buy as much as before, so they complained about how much tax you were asking. So, on an equal vote basis, you set up a system so that you take more from the people who could best afford it: the rich ones. This kind of income tax is called a "progressive tax." Now, a greater number of people are happy. The only ones who were less happy were the rich; and not only could they afford it, but when all the votes were counted, they had lost anyway.

Things were going along about like you would expect for a while. But then the rich people got together and came to you and said they felt the taxes were too high. You paid attention, because it looked like if you didn't, you might not get to keep your job. Then you noticed you had some extra cash on hand just in case someone else wanted to enter the game. Probably no one would notice if you gave some of that to the people who needed it. And anyway, since the game started, people had been checking in and out— and never did all the people check out at once—so you always had plenty of pennies. But somebody did notice and called your attention to the fact that the basic rules prohibited your spending anything you hadn't gotten from the players. (Article I, Section 9, Paragraph 7 of the Constitution). What you, as President, were doing was "inflating" the currency in the game. Since you couldn't continue to inflate directly, you had the Legislature create a new group, called the Federal Reserve Board (FRB), to be in charge of the cash. You told the FRB it really had to be honest with the cash system because it was so important. But then you set it up so that no one could check and see how it was doing. A few complained, but not too many people had read the rules. So it seemed to work pretty well.

Once in a while, someone who you didn't even know was in the game came to the FRB with $100 and asked for a penny. You found out that some of the players were having outsiders do some things for them. They were giving play money to the outsiders but told them that the FRB would give them a real penny if they had enough of the cash. And sure enough, it was true. And the FRB really didn't care too much because they had lots of pennies that had been turned in. And the game goes on.

This game-picture helps give a quite accurate conception of what inflation is. It is the increase of cash in the game for which no pennies have been turned in and for which no goods and services are coming to market. Inflation is a problem caused by cheating. Even if you set up guidelines for it, it is still cheating. The rules were set up so that Congress could establish the standards—that is, determine just what the "penny" would be. But the rules did not authorize any cheating by Congress (or anyone else). When you look at the other standards that Congress establishes—gallon, pound, yard, second, acre, etc.—you can easily see how it is necessary that no one be allowed to cheat. Our Constitution, in a key paragraph (Article I Section 8, Paragraph 5), charges Congress with the responsibility of coining money and regulating its value and fixing weights and measures.

Standards are necessary so that both parties to any transaction will know the exact meanings of the words they are using. With the standards established you know you can rely on them.

Every nation has a system of standard weights and measures which includes a standard-to-measure value. All standards have names. Our standard of value is named "dollar," and it has a definition. The current (1980) definition of a dollar is 1/42.22 ounces of gold or 412½ grains of silver, 9/10ths fine (pure). Congress has the Constitutional responsibility to establish that definition in either gold or silver and act on the definition. It acts on this by "coining" dollars or fractional dollars. For 150 years, no one had any real problem with the process. However, over the years, Congress has taken a series of steps—a little bit at a time—each step taking us slightly further from the Constitution until, at last, we now have no lawful "money" system at all, just paper and slugs in circulation. What we use instead of money can be called "currency." For quite a while, the currency was redeemable in silver or gold coins, but now all you can get for a $20 bill is smaller denominations notes, and if you ask for "hard money" you can get 20 Susan B. Anthony coins or other nickel/copper coins with not a trace of gold or silver in them. We are victims of fraud.[2]

This key section (Article I, Section 8, Paragraph 5) does not authorize Congress to circulate currency. Article I, Section 10, Paragraph 1, prohibits the States from coining money, circulating currency or making anything but gold and silver coin a tender in payment of debts. The 10th Amendment says (in full): "The powers not delegated to the United States by the Constitution, nor prohibited by it to the States, are reserved to the States respectively, or to the people." Taken together, these three parts mean, in essence, that the Federal government cannot circulate currency. Now, technically, the Federal government is not circulating currency. The Congress has created the Federal Reserve Board (a private agency) and given it the power to circulate currency. But how can Congress assign a privilege it does not have? Perhaps you could make a good case that there would be nothing wrong with this if the private agency were to keep its currency redeemable in "lawful money" and were subject to the laws of fraud. But the currency is **not** redeemable and the agency has not even been audited since its beginning, much less held accountable for its fraud.

Consider this parable. If a contractor agreed with the government to furnish 5,000 square feet of warehouse space for $50,000 but wanted to reserve the right to determine what "1 foot" meant, the government would righteously object, citing that key Constitutional paragraph in its objection. And it could get this objection enforced in the courts. But when the government fiddles with what "one dollar" means and the contractor objects, he has no place to turn. The contractor could not claim he could not furnish an honest foot "because he didn't have enough inches." Neither can the government claim it cannot furnish an honest currency standard because it will not abide by its own definition. I say the contractor, like any other citizen, can turn to the Constitution, to that same key paragraph, for his protection.

Or consider a small town that has only one gas station. The operator of the gas station changes the pump so that it delivers less gasoline, but the pump still says "one gallon" and charges the same price. If the one who is running the pump is also the one who decides what "one gallon" is, then you have a problem. That's why you need a Constitution.

Let's look at what "money" is. Basically, money is stored-up work. Money has several characteristics. One is that it is widely acceptable. Everyone wants the results of work. Another is that it is easily divisible. At one time, cows were used for money. But you can't divide them very well. That's one reason why cows didn't work too well as "money." Also, money is a good storage of value. That means it won't rust, melt or rot: And that's one reason we don't use salt as money as our ancestors did. Also, money is a standard unit of account. Lots of things have been used as money at one time or another, but 4,000 years of history show that the best money is gold. Gold is widely desired, can easily be cut into two, doesn't rot or rust or tarnish, and a specific amount of it is a dependable unit of account. In our Monopoly® game parallel, the penny is the money. The paper is the currency. Currency is used because it is a lot more convenient than money. Notes, checks and even electronic impulses can be used as currency. But to be honest, the currency must be redeemable in the money it represents. With a defined money you can have a paper currency exchangeable for it. But the paper is not identical to the money. Theoretically, you could have the paper redeemable in pork or potatoes. However, the Constitution (Article I, Section 10, Paragraph 1) requires the States to pay their bills with gold or silver coin, so I guess that's what the Founders meant for us to use.

For a currency to be honest it must be exchangeable for what it is proclaimed to be. A "note" is valid only if it can be redeemed. The Federal Reserve Note (FRN) cannot be redeemed; it has neither a "due date" nor a location. The creation of these "claims," representing neither money nor goods and services coming to market, is inflation. These extra claims dilute the other currency already issued. They compete in the marketplace for the goods and services already created and this necessarily results in price increases. The price increases are not the inflation; they are the result of the inflation. (Wet streets don't cause rain.)

Consider this idea. On an airplane trip we turn in our valuable suitcase, and we get back a piece of paper (claim check). Then, when we get to our destination,

we take this piece of paper, present it to the baggage clerk to claim the value it represents and get our fair share back. Similarly, when you do your job you get a claim check (currency) which you then take to the marketplace to exchange for your share of the things you and other productive people have created. How would you feel if, when you turned in your baggage check, the clerk said, "Oh, we need two baggage checks for each suitcase now. While you were out on your travels, someone printed some extra baggage checks, and so the only way we can make it come out even is to require you turn in two baggage checks for each suitcase." We could say the baggage clerk has raised the "price." But he has not personally caused inflation. The printing of fraudulent baggage checks is the "inflation." Similarly, Congress authorizes the printing of currency for which no work has been done, and puts it in circulation through their programs. This is exactly what is being done, and this is exactly what inflation is. But all the attention is misdirected to the resulting price increases, and people are unhappy with the baggage clerk, the store clerk, the gas station attendant or other salesman whose job requires they collect the price needed to cover the inflated costs.

Incidentally, I looked very carefully at the Constitution and there **IS NOT** a section which says, "If any part of this document is inconvenient or difficult to comply with, it may be ignored." Further, George Washington, in his farewell address said: "The basis of our political systems is the right of the **people** to make and to alter their constitutions of government. But the constitution which at any time exists, till changed by an explicit and authentic act of the whole people, is sacredly obligatory upon all." But we can ignore this because George was kind of old-fashioned since he believed in honesty, integrity, principle, patriotism and responsibility—words that have since been put in museums as curios of an earlier age. Anyway, shouldn't the Constitution adapt to changing times? After all, "Big Mother" government knows what's best for you, and if you don't agree, "Big Brother" government will help you change your mind.

Remember the good old days when the dollar bill said, "This certifies there is on deposit in the U.S. Treasury one Dollar in silver payable to the bearer on demand," and they meant it? Now they just ignore it. The dollar bill just says this is "legal tender," which means you can use it to pay your bills. If you think of a checking account, it's easy to see you can't issue checks for more than you have in the account. But the FRNs represent a piece of the national debt, not money in the bank.

Suppose my house were worth $20,000 and I sold 1,000 shares in it. Each share would be worth $20. But if I printed additional "shares" that looked the same as the original shares and sold them, that would be fraudulent. The additional shares would assume the appearance of value only as they diluted the value of the original shares. That would be "inflation." If you could not check on how many shares I had sold, you would not be able to confirm the fraud. Others being asked to accept these shares in a trade would notice that there were more of them around than there used to be, so they would ask for a greater number in exchange for what they had to offer. That would be a "price increase." Now, if I took a big mortgage out on my house and didn't tell you about it, that, too, would be fraudulent. If I sold the house and just left you with a share of the mortgage, that would be an additional fraud. A share of my house is a share of an asset; a share of the mortgage is a share of a liability, and is quite a different thing. Forcing you to take shares in my mortgage as "payment" for working for me would be more descriptive of how it REALLY is. But that's not all. To be like our government, we need to do more.

We need to set up a tax structure which penalizes you if you try to earn more in an attempt to keep even with the price increases. This is called the "progressive income tax." That little piece of paper, FRN represents a piece of the debt which they forced you to loan to the FRB and on which they are taxing you to pay the interest. In this Alice-in-Wonderland situation, the more they wring out of you the better off they say you are. At the present time, Congress borrows from you to finance their deficit spending and this borrowing creates inflation which **results** in price increases which you also have to pay. Studies indicate that a 10 percent inflation rate results in approximately a 16 percent increase in government tax receipts. This inflation increases taxes without ever recording a vote. This process is called the "fiscal dividend." This year (1980), this part of the **unlegislated** tax increase is about $10 billion, or about $300 per family, and is expected to be $16 billion next year.[3]

Inflation has a long and sordid history. It is cited as one of the chief reasons for the fall of the Roman Empire. It is a reflection of the government's decision to cheat, and the mechanism soon spreads the incentive to cheat to all throughout the land. The glowing counter-example is the Byzantine Empire, which maintained the purity of its gold coinage for 800 years. It fell only after it failed to honor the world's trust in its money. Inflation, as we now have, has a nearly perfect record as a destroyer of civilizations. I am aware of only one exception: West Germany. Though it had been urged by our government to inflate its currency, (in 1948) it decided not to. The Germans had been down that inflation road in the 1920s and didn't need to travel it again. If they can establish sound money, we can do it, too. But we don't need their example. Our constitution has the restraints designed to keep the money sound. It's just that these restraints are being ignored.

Ignoring these restraints was not accidental. It was carefully planned. Rexford Tugwell, part of Franklin D. Roosevelt's "Brain Trust," wrote: "(these government actions) were tortured interpretations of (the Constitution) intended to prevent them... But it really had to be admitted that it was done irregularly and according to doctrines the farmers would have rejected. ...Much of the (apparent) lagging and reluctance was owed to constantly reiterated intention that it was done in pursuit of the aims embodied in the Constitution of 1787, when obviously it was in contravention of them." To this, William Simon, Treasury

Secretary 1974-1977, adds: "Tugwell was saying here, in the plainest possible English, that there was only one way to force FDR's economic collectivism into our political system, and that was to violate the Constitution. And because it required a violation of the Constitution, the New Dealers found it necessary to lie about their goals and to pretend that they were conforming to the Constitution. That is the genesis of the doublespeak that still addles Americans' brains and allows them to describe a continuous invasion of individual rights and liberty as the enhancement of freedom."[4]

A financial "note" is a promise to pay. When it has been fulfilled, you have been paid. If it is not fulfilled, you have not been paid. The Treasury note redeemable for one dollar in silver is a good example of a valid note. That currency was redeemable in an asset (silver). To say that a "promise to pay" has been redeemed when you get for it another "promise to pay" puts you in an endless circle. This is equivalent to saying that a "promise to pay" is the same as a "promise not to pay." Black is not white. Even if a motion is made that it should be and a majority vote in favor of it, it still isn't.

The FRNs have a face amount equal to the bonds they represent. This is called "monetizing the debt." But currency backed by a debt is a mirage. The currency is not an "I.O.U." It's a "U-O-Me." It represents the promise of the government to extort value from the producers in the future.

Consider the relationship between the fraudulent currency and the progressive income tax. It's like a government agent sneaking into your house and stealing from your cookie jar. But you didn't see him take the cash, you just noted that some was gone. So you work extra hard to make up for it and are penalized by the income tax structure for the extra work. It's as though the government agent commits a crime and then penalizes YOU as an accessory because you didn't stop it. We don't even have a word for such an action. Since millions are being defrauded this way, I suggest the word MEGAFRAUD.

The government has built a "house of cards" on a "foundation of sand." The house of cards is our present currency structure, and the foundation of sand is the belief that no one would ever figure out what they have done and what could be done about it.

CHAPTER II

How Did it Happen?

Inflation is not new. Its seeds are deep within us and all around. It springs from the universal wish to get something for nothing. Even the fox catching a chicken is appropriating something that was not his. Politicians are even slicker than the fox. They make the chickens think they are being benefited. Anyway, they try not to kill the chickens; they go for the eggs. The eggs are useful to get other things. They need the chickens. If they killed the chickens, there wouldn't be any eggs; and then the politicians might have to scratch around a bit. They don't want to do that; it looks too much like work. The politicians' hunger for eggs is unlimited, so they keep taking more and more of them. If the chickens notice and squawk, then the politicians promise to take fewer eggs next year. That's called a "tax reduction." If there really aren't enough eggs to go around, the politicians encourage the chickens to work harder. That's called "growth," and everyone knows that's good. If a chicken finds a hole in the fence and lays some eggs that hatch so the chicken has a little brood of her own, that's called a "loophole" and is immediately closed when found, because everyone knows loopholes are bad. Some chickens don't scratch around enough to lay usable eggs, so the politicians take a few extra from the other hens so they will have some to share. That's called "transfer payments." What I have described is not inflation, it's just the tax structure.

Inflation comes into the picture because the politicians

have figured it's hazardous to their health to raise taxes as high as they would like them. So in addition to the tax, they introduce cheating. To introduce inflation, the politicians require the chickens leave their eggs in storage under the politicians' care. In exchange for the eggs they get receipts, each one good for one egg. Here we are back to paper again. The politicians find they can get work done with payments in receipts rather than actual eggs. The first thing you know they're putting out more "receipts" than they have eggs. That's inflation! Of course, some of the chickens might want to redeem their receipts. But this is taken care of by making it illegal to redeem the receipts. Now, inflation is installed in the system.

President Thomas Jefferson once said, "A private central bank issuing the public currency is a greater menace to the liberties of the people than a standing army." Now, we are getting a better idea of what he meant.

The framers of the Constitution apparently did not believe the States could be trusted to print *currency or coin money*, so those actions are prohibited (Article I, Section 10, Paragraph 1). It is mentioned that Congress shall fix standards and coin money (Article I, Section 8, Paragraph 5), but it is not mentioned that Congress may print currency. The 10th Amendment seems to "tie it up" by stating that those things not specified are reserved to the people. A hundred years ago, the railroads and banks printed currency, so private currency is not a new idea. It was nearly 200 years ago when Chief Justice John Marshall, in the case of *Maryland v. McCullough*, stated that the printing of currency is incidental to the coining of money, which means that as long as Congress is authorized to coin money it is necessarily included in that power that they can print currency. However, this opinion did not amend the Constitution. I believe I have shown this (and related) decisions to be wrong. They are based on the presumption that the government would not cheat. You have only to look at the irredeemable paper and base-metal slugs in your possession to see what has been done. You have been defrauded. It is a MEGAFRAUD!

If I were to defraud you, you could call down upon me an entire group of laws fully enforceable by the courts to rectify things. But if the government itself defrauds you, where do you turn? I believe the Constitution is the place. Perhaps I am wrong. But no one has shown me a single significant point in which I am in error. If you can find an error, I ask you to let me know.

Both the Federal Reserve Board and the progressive income tax were instituted in 1913. The income tax affected fewer than 1 percent of the people. That meant that 99 percent couldn't care less. And anyway, the wealthy could afford it. Things really did not get organized until the Presidency of Franklin D. Roosevelt. He was elected on a program and a promise to reduce the government spending. He was committed to the gold standard, balancing the budget and many other things that sounded very good and which were written into the Democrat Party's platform. However, immediately upon his being elected, he reversed his position and made holding our money, that is our own gold, illegal. He closed all the banks and then decided on the basis of good politics which ones would be allowed to open. What a way to control! This action cut the taproot connection with the Constitution, and it has been downhill ever since. Oh, there have been different slopes down the hill from time to time, but downhill it is. Some of the programs he instituted were challenged in the courts. When a program was overruled by the Supreme Court, he threatened to "pack" the Supreme Court by adding a dozen additional men to it who would support his programs. This proposal would have made the courts of law instruments of lawlessness.

In the face of this the Supreme Court's hands were tied. Congress was so responsive to this very strong leader that it literally passed bills that were only titles, with the content to be written later in the White House. With the borrow-and-inflate, tax-and-spend system so thoroughly developed under Roosevelt's administration, it is easy to see how it would continue. It is as addictive as it is destructive.

One of the essential things for the government to do is to divert attention from the real source of the problem. If you can keep people concerned about the results and never let them realize the source, then they stay occupied but can never solve anything. You see, you can never solve a problem by working on the results. No matter how much you mop the streets, it doesn't stop the rain. One of the basic ways to conceal the real problem is to give it the wrong name. You define the result of the problem as the problem itself, and that makes it very hard for people to figure out. In this case, you define inflation as rising prices. THEN you just watch and see who raises their prices, and LO AND BEHOLD, they are responsible for "inflation." It's the people spending too much; it's the businessman raising his price to cover his cost; it's the laborer asking for a wage increase to offset his increased bills; it's—well you can fill in the blank.

Thirty years ago, when I was in the army, I was told the country's gold-flow problem was my fault and to correct it I should buy only in the Post Exchange. I didn't cause it; how can I solve it? I didn't make the cash rotten; they did.

Of course, the ultimate irony is when you have a government program that is causing a problem, you attack the problem with another government program. In this case, you attack the rising prices which are caused by the government destruction of the currency by a program making it illegal to increase prices. This is somewhat

THE LONG ARM OF THE CONGRESS

analogous to seeing that sickness is usually related to an increased temperature and deciding to "cure" sickness by making a law that no thermometer can read higher than 98.6° F. Wage and price controls have a perfect record of failure, but that doesn't keep politicians from trying. All of the programs cost money, but it's very easy to appear saintly with someone else's cash.

A startling true story on this point of someone else's cash is reported from *The Life of Colonel David Crockett* in a recent magazine.[5]

Though the story is too long to reproduce here, I highly recommend it since it exposes like a flash of lightning how our Constitutional situation has changed in 177 years. In the story, Davy Crockett, as a U.S. Representative, is confronted by a voter dissatisfied with Crockett's approving funds for victims of a fire.

The voter, Horatio Bunce, makes the following points: "...the Constitution, to be worth anything, must be held sacred, and rigidly observed in all its provisions. *The man who wields power and misinterprets it is the more dangerous the more honest he is*... The power of collecting and disbursing money at pleasure is the most dangerous power that can be entrusted to man, particularly under our system of collecting revenue by a tariff, which reaches every man in the country, no matter how poor he may be... If you had the right to give anything, the amount was simply a matter of discretion with you, and you had as much right to give $20,000,000 as $20,000. If you have the right to give to one, you have the right to give to all; and as the Constitution neither defines charity nor stipulates the amount, you are at liberty to give to any and everything which you may believe, or profess to believe, is a charity, and to any amount you may think proper. You will very easily perceive what a wide door this would open for fraud and corruption and favoritism, on the one hand, and for robbing the people on the other. ...Individual members may give as much of their own money as they please, but they have no right to touch a dollar of the public money for that purpose... The people have delegated to Congress, by the Constitution, the power to do certain things. To do these, it is authorized to collect and pay moneys, and for nothing else. Everything beyond this is usurpation, and a violation of the Constitution."

Davy Crockett is greatly moved by the discussion and

later offers his own money to worthy victims and challenges other Congressmen to also donate. However, the difference between their money and public money is great, Crockett relates... "[N]ot one of them responded to my proposition. Money with them is nothing but trash when it is to come out of the people. But, it is the one great thing for which most of them are striving and many of them sacrifice honor, integrity, and justice to obtain it."

Things haven't changed much. That was written at a time when at least the money was honest. Now with the money not even being honest the contrast is more devastating. You can look around and see how much cash has flowed wrongfully through this fraudulent "door" in the Constitution.

CHAPTER III

What Difference Does it Make?

The briefest response to what difference inflation makes is to ask yourself what difference a little bit of cancer makes. At first, you hardly notice it. But if you don't stop it, it keeps growing and growing until finally you are dead. Besides, this cancer is contagious.

Since money is a standard, distorting it leads to distorting everything measured with it. In our particular case it is the interaction with the progressive income tax I feel is particularly vicious. The **average** tax you pay is a particular percent (total tax divided by total income). If you earn an additional $100, the **extra** tax you pay on that $100 is the **marginal** tax percent. The marginal tax percent is always higher than the average tax percent. This slight increase in tax rate leads to what is called the "fiscal dividend." As mentioned before, if the government causes 10 percent inflation and you work extra to offset it, the taxes go up about 16 percent. This is why when you get a "cost-of-living" raise, your check reads higher numbers, but you have more month left at the end of the money. Look at what happens to a 6 percent savings account with 6 percent inflation. First, you pay tax on the 6 percent interest; typically about 30 percent (your marginal tax rate), so you keep only about 4.2 percent. Second, the 6 percent "inflation" affects not only your interest, **but the entire account.** So you multiply the basic account (plus interest, after taxes) by .94 and you have a **total** of .9794 of whatever you started off with the year before (1.0000). The value loss has evaporated into the government's sponge. You feel ahead because the numbers are bigger, but you are behind because what's left buys less. With higher numbers you lose more, with smaller numbers you lose less. But **you always** lose. MEGAFRAUD!

Or consider a house you had bought and paid for 20 years ago, costing $20,000. You own it "free and clear." At that time the currency was redeemable in silver. Now the currency is redeemable in nothing and worth about one-fifth of what it was 20 years ago. So the "price" of the same house is $100,000. But if you sell the house using the depreciated currency you have a "capital gains" tax to pay. That's **your** penalty, because **they** have destroyed the currency. It's that MEGAFRAUD again. Twenty years ago, the government had no claim on your home; they now claim a substantial chunk of it, and you can go to jail if you don't pay it. (Maybe MEGAFRAUD isn't a strong enough word.)

One of the characteristics of money is that it is a good storage of value. Depreciating currency doesn't act that way. The value just rots away as you hold it. Last year, the rate of rotting got to one-tenth of 1 percent every 48 hours. Officially stated, that's 1.5 percent per month.

Consider the businessman who is depreciating some equipment or buildings. As the "write-off" is spread over a number of years, but limited to the original cost of the item, there is never enough at the end of the period to replace the used-up thing. This means that part of the profits was phantom profit, but it is taxed for real. I read a report that said that if the nation's railroads were allowed honest depreciation and the real taxes on phantom profits

returned, **all** the taxes they had paid in 75 years would have to be returned. The railroads would be fully solvent. It is a serious problem.

One of the problems with being paid in irredeemable receipts of declining value is that you are trapped to the extent that if you hold them you will immediately and continuously lose. This means that even holding currency is a speculation, and a losing one at that, as everyone knows who has held a savings account or fixed-income investment over the past few years. You save some cash, hoping to sit in your easy chair and quietly enjoy your savings. Then you find someone is pushing your chair down a super-highway at great speed through risky traffic. This continuous loss in value discourages true savings and investments, which are the only basis for sound economic growth.

How much has this fraudulent Federal currency scheme already cost you? According to the American Institute for Economic Research Bulletin of March 1980, the cost since 1939 is $3,185,700,000,000. That's more than $3 trillion and is too big a number to be easily understood. Broken down, it averages more than $5 per family **per day.** This is the theft first spoken of in Chapter I. They also state that over the past 10 years, the theft through inflation has equaled the **total** of the individual income taxes paid during that period.

In the drive to collect all possible taxes, it is easy for the government to treat your Constitutional rights lightly. Usually you can depend on the courts to affirm what the Constitution says, but there is a recent Supreme Court ruling that concerns me. Previously they had held that the IRS could not violate your rights against unlawful search and seizure and then use the evidence to convict you. In this recent case they said it was all right for the IRS to hire someone else to violate your rights and **then** use the evidence to convict you. To say that sets a dangerous precedent would be an understatement.[6]

Of course, the Siren Song will be sung: After all, he was a criminal, wasn't he? You can relax, you're in good hands. Anyway, it wasn't your briefcase they went through and photographed.

Some might say that our government experts know best. They know just how much fraudulent currency to create each week or month. They even have a nice name for it—it's called "fine-tuning." But it is still cheating. If an individual wants to do the things that lead to bankruptcy, that is his decision, and he must be responsible for it. But I do not accept that the people in Washington have a right to do things that will drive our entire country into bankruptcy. That becomes my concern. There are many people in this country trying to extend this fraudulent currency system to the international sphere through the International Monetary Fund (IMF). But our Constitution does not give them the authority to hand control of our currency to the IMF. Hopefully, the Constitution means something. It is the only Constitution of which I am aware that speaks directly to this way of defrauding. It has been overlooked, avoided and ignored far too long.

Someone commented to me that things weren't working all that badly. I replied that he reminded me of a man who jumped off the Empire State Building. All the way down people heard him say as he went by their window, "So far, so good." Senator Barry Goldwater stated that the country is in the weakest economic and military situation that it has been in more than 200 years.

One of the biggest changes that honest currency would mean would be that the tax structure would have to be honest. That would make the total tax load visible, and then you could see that you are spending more than 40 percent of your time feeding the system. One indication of the difficulty of changing things is that another report I read indicated that more than 70 percent of the people (including dependents) get a monthly check or regular direct support from the government. Any suggestion for some kind of honesty immediately evokes the response that you are going to be taking food out of the mouths of the poor, the ones who can least afford it. That sounds appropriate until you divide the amount of cash sent their direction by the number of people it is aimed at. That comes out to about $20,000 per person. That number is far higher than the average income of the working person. You ask the person who is against honest currency just where the government should stop taking for redistribution and the answer is always, "We need more." We are tricked into playing a game—you could call it "Gotcha." We are asked to vote for candidates because they say they will make our neighbors do what we want them to do. Then after the election we are being forced to do what our neighbors want. I say the Constitution limits what my neighbors (through the government) can force me to do. It is no longer a game.

I looked more deeply into the "progressive tax structure," also referred to as "taxing according to the ability to pay," or "achieving vertical equity." This system is based technically on what is called the "declining marginal utility theory." What this theory basically says is that if you already have one of something—let's say a car—then another one isn't worth as much to you as the first. And if you have two cars, a third one isn't worth as much as the second car, and so forth. And this does apply with respect to "things." However, it does **not** apply with respect to **capabilities** that have a potential. If a person has six years of education, the value of the seventh year is higher than the sixth. If you have seven years of education, the value of the eighth is higher than the seventh, and so forth. The education represents a capability to make a meaningful decision, and everyone wants more capability. Another example is power. If you have a little bit and can measure a unit, an extra unit is worth more to seek than the last unit you obtained. And if you get that extra unit, an additional unit is desired even more. And this does hold consistently. This is obviously true; otherwise, the President and Congressmen, who already have a lot of power, wouldn't want any more. But see how they run! Because these assets represent a **potential** to make more decisions, they are increasingly desired; whereas a "thing" you already have represents a decision already made.

To apply the concept of "declining marginal utility" to a "$100 bill," for instance, assumes that it is a "thing" and that if you have one, another one will not be valued as highly. But a $100 bill is not a "thing;" it is a **capability.** It does not represent a decision made; it represents the capability to make a decision. No one, least of all a politician, is really in a position to say in great detail that this $100 bill has a greater value to the rich person than it does to the poor (or the reverse); that is for each to decide. But let's look at it from a different angle—what is technically called the "opportunity cost," or "opportunity value" of this particular item. This concept is one way we **can** look at value and we can establish guidelines or limits on the value a person places on some item by seeing what that person will give up for it (or will not give up for it).

There was a story in *The Wall Street Journal* that was particularly appropriate on this point. It was about one of the Rockefeller grandsons who was heir to dozens of millions of dollars. I would consider him rich. At this particular time, he was going to college, taking engineering. Their engineering activities were going to take them out into the field where they would be away from the town, the restaurants and other facilities. So the night before, this young fellow got the things to make sandwiches, bought soft drinks and snacks and carried them with him so that he might sell them to the other students to earn some additional income. I found it very interesting that he went to so much trouble to earn some additional income when he already had so much money. The opportunity to earn, say $100, was worth enough to him to give up the time it took and accept the risk of obtaining salable assets in advance. All of this was done in expectation that his potential customers would be willing to buy his merchandise so that he would end up with extra income (profit) after paying all the costs and creating that income. Our present tax structure penalizes people who do things like that. The typical fine (tax) for earning an extra $100 is greater than for running a traffic light.

Now let's look at what a poor person will do or give up to get the $100. (I would in advance agree that the poor person would "appreciate" and quickly use the $100.) The question though, is: What value would he put on the $100? Answer this by noting what he will give up in order to obtain the $100. My experience has been that the people whom we consider poor will not give up very much for the extra income. They will not leave the television set; they will **not** skip their bowling night; they will not give up their beer or their cigarettes; they will not work in an effective fashion to earn an extra income. Some will not even shave or wash. I am not saying that they must do these things; I am merely recognizing that this is the way things are. Typically, they are trying to do the least possible to get what could only be called a "free lunch." Our present economic structure subsidizes people who act this way. I am saying government should NOT give them things. It should make it easy for them to get a job and not penalize them if they do. We as individuals may certainly give things, but it should be out of our own pocket. God tells us to help the poor and needy. You and I, and nearly everyone else, have given help to unfortunate people. But we must be careful not to encourage people to be poor. Many people now are better off not working than they are when they do work. Do you think everybody agrees with the present system of welfare? I think it's wrong to extort value from the producers under threat of imprisonment (our present taxing system) in order to give it to people who have little or no economic incentive to work. Our present system penalizes people who work and subsidizes those who don't. Economically, I feel that this is why some people are poor, but that's not really the point. The point is, what a $100 bill is worth to a person is adequately measured by what he will give up for it, and I find that a poor person really won't give up much of anything for it. Whereas the person who is already better off or who chooses to work to become better off will give up a full $100 worth of value in order that this value may be converted into cash. The productive type of person would end up with cash which, to them, is an opportunity to make more meaningful decisions.

For reasons like this, the entire basis of taxing-according-to-the-ability-to-pay is wrong. Are we stuck with this system? A key question is: Which group do you want to encourage, those who make things and help our standard of living or those who do little or nothing and push to use things made by others?

We fought the Revolutionary War to rid ourselves of a despot controlling us from England. I doubt very much if the Founding Fathers fought that war so that the despot would move to Washington. But that is what we now have: an elected despot in Washington. How do I know that? Listen to this quote from William Pitt, the Earl of Chatham, England, speaking for the English despot. King George. "Let the sovereign authority of this country (England) over the colonies be asserted in as strong terms as can be assigned and be made to extend to every point of legislation whatsoever. That we may bind their trade, confine their manufactures, and exercise every power whatsoever, except that of taking their money out of their pockets without their own consent."[7] You see, we now have **all** those things of which the despot spoke, **plus** "the taking of money out of their pockets without their own consent." That's where the $5 went. It is this last MEGAFRAUD that is my primary concern.

A little saying I heard some time ago comes to mind: "If you don't change what you're doing, you're going to end up where you're headed."

CHAPTER IV

What Can Be Done About it?

The problems described seem so incredibly broad and complex that at first one is nearly overwhelmed at the difficulty of doing anything about them. That's the way I felt, but then I realized this is exactly the reaction the politicians want us to have. You see, if all who are not on the "take" are so overwhelmed that they don't know where to start, no start is ever made and nothing is ever done. You don't know whom to sue or what to do. That has been the case for 50 years.

My approach is different. My plan for working toward a solution is startling in its simplicity; it amounts to strictly abiding by the Constitution. Instead of trying to force Congress into complying with the Constitution, I decided to comply with the Constitution. Abiding by the Constitution is a **right** I have.[8] Anyone may comply with the Constitution. For three years, I have been issuing and circulating honest, redeemable $20 bills. I am **not** printing money; the **backing** is money, the paper is currency.[9] The bill carries a promise similar to our national currency of 50 years ago: "Redeemable in gold coin by bearer on demand." The gold coin, also known as a "double eagle," is the Constitutionally authorized, Congressionally approved coin minted when our dollar was defined as "one-twentieth of an ounce of gold, nine-tenths fine." This is a honest and Constitutional definition. Congress has the responsibility of determining the money standard, and this was the standard for more than 100 years. They have the mandate to "coin" money and for 100 years did just that—take one-twentieth of an ounce of gold and coin a dollar, or take one ounce of gold and coin $20. Since the greatest value was coined in the $20 denomination, I backed my currency with them. My currency is a "bill of credit;" that is, I owe the rightful owner $20. It is redeemable in gold coin. The only lawful $20 gold coin is one authorized by the Constitution and approved by Congress. That's what you get.

It should be noted that creating currency is not unique. Every time you write a check, you are creating currency. Every time you sign a credit slip, you are creating currency. Every time you buy a money order, new currency is created. Mine is different only in that it is redeemable honestly. With mine you get Constitutional money; with others you get "phony money."

Economists will tell you there's not enough gold for honest currency. But that is not true. The Byzantine Empire maintained the purity of their gold money for 800 years, and only fell after it failed to honor the world's trust in its money. There is enough gold for **honest** currency, there is not (and never can be) enough gold (or anything else) to back **dishonest** currency. Gold is not what is lacking, it is honesty.

You can buy my private currency and can get the price by writing or calling for a quote. You can estimate the price pretty well because its price is what it costs to buy the backing, plus a small service charge (less than 5 percent). There is no charge for redemption. If you pay for it with gold coins, there is no charge at all.[10]

My performing with currency is Constitutional. (The accuracy of my opinion has essentially been confirmed by the government itself. In 1977, shortly after I started, the Treasury Department had the Secret Service investigate my activity and they found nothing objectionable.) You, as a citizen, have a right to nothing less. But if my performance **is** Constitutional, what the government is doing is **something else.** It's MEGAFRAUD again. The Constitution is not written in Greek or Latin, it is written in English. You should read it for yourself. It takes only about 20 minutes. It is based on freedom and responsibility and has as its aim establishing limits on what the government may do. Thirty years ago, as a West Point graduate, I swore to "support and defend the Constitution against all enemies, foreign and domestic." That is my goal. You should know that every government officer (legislative, executive and judicial) and employee has taken the equivalent oath. Sometimes, the way they treat it you would think that "support and defend" the Constitution means providing a table for the **document** and posting a guard (which they do).

If I can comply with the Constitution, why can't Congress? Simple. It can, but it doesn't want to. In a parallel example, for three years, President Jimmy Carter said it was impossible to balance the Federal budget. Early in 1980, it became politically popular to balance the budget. Then, it took about three weeks to issue a balanced budget. Don't get me wrong — it's balanced with mirrors and more fraud. The assumptions about income are increased; the assumptions about expenses are reduced. It will not hold up. But the important point is that the budget action conclusively shows that previously they didn't want to balance it. (They still don't, but at least now they **say** they are trying.)

We didn't get to our present set of difficulties overnight. It took about 50 years of concerted effort, twisting the Constitution out of shape. You can imagine horror stories of the chaos if we instantly went back to what we had 50 years ago. I agree: That would be a problem. But consider the reverse. Imagine yourself proposing 50 years ago that the government take approximately 50 percent of the **gross** income and dissipate it while converting our nation from the highest to the lowest growth rate among the developed countries. That exposure of the intended path would have resulted in immediate rejection; the big-government advocates know that and, therefore, concealed it. I am saying, "Reverse the present process. Make your decisions and actions in accordance with the Constitution."

There's a story appropriate to illustrate this point. If you take a frog and put him in a pan of hot water, he will jump right out. To stay would be fatal. But if you take the same frog and put him in a pan of cold water, he will stay. If you then put a small flame under the pan, it will slowly heat up. You can kill the frog this way, because he can never figure out just when he **has** to jump out to save his life. In a similar fashion, the destructive fires are heating up our situation, but indecision and fear are paralyzing people.

I say the irredeemable currency is a **key** part of the heat that's "cooking our goose." With it, Congress is cheating me. They have no Constitutional (or other) authority for cheating me. I'm telling them to stop it. One person said, "But aren't they cheating everybody?" And I replied, "I know of no situation where you catch someone cheating that it is an adequate defense to say:

Federal Reserve Note
Honest when printed—Dishonest now.

'I'm trying to cheat everyone equally.'" If you think I'm wrong, show me.

Some Congressmen (or others) might say that "overall," people agree with the present system. If you think that's true, consider a small amendment to the income tax laws: "From now on, the budget will be broken down according to the various percentages spent in each of the several areas. If you disagree with any of the expenditures, you may reduce or increase your tax for that particular percentage." To even consider such an amendment briefly shows what would follow. The amounts discarded by the people expected to pay for it would boggle your mind. They do **not** agree with the present system. They are intentionally prevented from becoming aware of the MEGAFRAUD. (Technically "covering up" a felony is a crime called "misprision of a felony," but don't expect anyone to be indicted on that one.)

Others might say, "Well, let's change the Constitution." After all, it can be amended, and the amendment applies if three-fourths of the States confirm it. OK. Consider how you would write the amendments to cover the present situation. How about: "If any part of this document is inconvenient or difficult to comply with, it may be ignored." Or: "The Government may cheat any one person or group of people as much as it wants without limit." Outrageous? Of course. But that's how it would have to read to cover the present circumstances. Of course, the government should not steal. Well, how about half-steal?

You, I and nearly everyone else have "had one slipped over us." We have been told that a "promise to pay" (note) is redeemed when we get for it another "promise to pay." Promises, promises, but never any performance.

A little more technical discussion is appropriate here. It is worth noting that if a law is passed which is counter to the Constitution, legally **it is as if that law had never been passed.** It should also be noted that the "claim and exercise of a Constitutional right cannot be converted into a crime." (*Miller v U.S.* 230F486 at 489). You should also note that the 9th Amendment states in full: "The enumeration in the Constitution, of certain rights, shall not be construed to deny or disparage others retained by the people." This means that if our forefathers had a **right** to do a thing before the Constitution, the Constitution did not take that **right** away.[11] Further, the government cannot license or tax your Constitutional rights, for it is well known that, "The power to tax is the power to destroy." (As noted in *Miranda v Arizona* 380 US 436 1966, "where fundamental rights under the Constitution are involved there can be no rule-making or legislation which can abrogate them.")

Some might ask, "But Congress means well, and besides, what can one person do?" Well, an individual can do great things, but their motives are important. Consider a combat situation with Andy, Bob and Chuck. A live grenade comes in, and Andy decides to throw himself on it. That will save Bob and Chuck. That is an act of great courage and valor. Men have gotten the Congressional Medal of

Honor for just that. We have no higher award for the action following the decision that, "This should be done, and I will do it." But notice the shift that occurs in the same situation if Andy decides, "This should be done" and he picks up Chuck and puts **him** on the grenade. This is quite different. Andy wants to use Chuck to save himself. The difference is not changed if Andy gets Bob's help to put Chuck on the grenade, pointing out it will save Bob too. It is not changed (assuming there were time) if they vote on it and **then** put Chuck on the grenade. (After all, I'm sure he would be out-voted 2-1.) Andy and Bob do not have the right to put Chuck on the grenade. As a group, we do not have the right to put any person on the grenade. Majority vote does not go this far.

We have difficult problems as a nation. All people do. Some might even be thought of as "time bombs." I might decide to do something about them. But that does not give me the right to decide my companion must do something about them for me. He does not belong to me, and I may not make that decision for him. Yet financially, we are doing exactly that. We, as "A" and "B" get together and decide what sacrifice "C" must make for "D." "D" may be deserving and all that, and we might think "C" can afford it, but "C" is not ours to divide up. Majority rule does not extend that far. (Incidentally, "A" is the Administration, "B" is the Congress. "C" is anyone who does anything economically productive, and "D" is who gets the checks, food stamps, etc.) The sneaky thing is that "A" and "B" can depend on "D" to approve their actions since it's somebody else's cash. "Money from the government is free, isn't it?" As I said before, it's fun to be generous with other people's money. It's also wrong. Since the number of "Ds" who vote exceed the number of "Cs" who vote, the system is now in a tailspin. "A" and "B" are working hard to increase the number of "Ds" (currently about 70 percent of the total population) while attempting to conceal from "Cs" what is going on. The vicious thing is how this process destroys "D" by encouraging and paying for self-destructive behavior. This is what our government has done and is doing. The government is succeeding. It is intentional.

But even more than that, it is so frightened at how great a sacrifice, how high a price, it is extorting from "C," that it conceals the price. **Planned inflation is a key part of the concealment.** Income tax is the visible price, and it is bad enough to create complaints. The vast multitude of hidden taxes are an even higher price (in total, **twice the size of the income tax)** and are levied on producers who must collect them when any goods or services are sold. Even this is not enough; the fraud of inflation is **intentionally** created and released to silently devour the substance of the people so that even more value is sucked to Washington. Even greater sacrifices are silently enforced. This great system of unlegislated tax increases is now fully in place. It is going to extort an estimated $109 billion during the coming year (1981), which amounts to more than $2,000 per family. (The so-called "tax reduction" being talked about is not a tax cut at all, but would just limit the increase to perhaps $80 billion.) This is so much additional tax that, along with underestimating the expenses and overestimating the income, Congress is proclaiming that it is "balancing the budget." **Hypocrite** is not a strong-enough word for Congress; we need a stronger one.

Here it is appropriate to mention the biggest incentive the government has for an unConstitutional currency: It has an essential interaction with the tax structure to wring more value out of you. Since the first edition of this book, some readers pointed out—and my study confirmed—that the present collection of income tax from individuals not engaged in the exercise of a privilege is unConstitutional.

I am not an attorney, so please don't consider my remarks a **legal** opinion. But note, as a matter of fact, each seems to require the other. These tax points are not my primary concern, but I believe they should have the greatest possible notoriety. Even with the 16th Amendment, the Constitution authorizes only two kinds of personal tax: direct and indirect. The direct taxes must be by apportionment, which means everybody's taxes must be the same amount. The indirect tax must be the taxing of a **privilege.** In indirect taxes, the rule is uniformity. The 16th Amendment was specifically concerned with an excise tax on the privilege of corporate activity.

The present income tax is a personal tax. It is collected as a direct tax, yet it is obviously not apportioned equally. Therefore, it is not Constitutional as a direct tax. If it is to be Constitutional as an **indirect tax,** one must ask what privilege is being taxed. That must be the **privilege of working. But working is not a privilege, it is a right.** And rights may not be taxed. (Note the 9th Amendment previously mentioned.) So it is not Constitutional as an indirect tax. There is no other choice. It's MEGAFRAUD again.

Is your position privileged? You have a common-law **right** to work, and that right may not be Constitutionally taxed. When you trade your time for cash, that is **wage.** Wages are not income. Income is the profit or gain earned in the exercise of a privilege. At the present time, the categories regarded as privileged are corporations, attorneys and criminals. The Constitution (9th Amendment) specifically preserves unnamed rights for the citizens. The government cannot license or tax your Constitutional rights since "the power to tax is the power to destroy." Our forefathers had the **right** to be in business as individuals; the stories of the wagon-peddler are widespread.

Yet this type of activity is now taxed.

Another substantial point concerns the 5th Amendment. No one may be required to be a witness against himself. Yet the entire income tax is based on the presumption that you will waive this right. The Supreme Court has confirmed that you **have** this right with respect to the tax return. (*Garner vs. U.S.*, 424 U.S. 648; *Hale vs. Henkel*, 201 U.S. 43). Yet the IRS would have you believe you will go to jail if you do not become a witness against yourself. It's MEGAFRAUD again.

Also consider this. The IRS taxes dollar income. But what is a dollar? I claim it is what the law says it is: 1/42.22 ounce of gold or 412.5 grains of silver, nine-tenths fine. The statutes hold that a promise to perform is not a performance. A promise to pay is not payment. Yet the tax court held that receiving a private agency's (Federal Reserve Board) irredeemable note, which no longer promises anything, is the same as getting the gold or silver. If that's true, then receiving a note which is redeemable in gold or silver has to be equivalent to theirs. But they are as different as night and day. As of this writing, it takes about 50 of their $20 bills to be equivalent to one of mine. Equal? Hardly. MEGAFRAUD!

Recalling the big "Monopoly®" game described earlier, the players may turn in $100 play money to get their penny back. But the banker (FRB), having cheated, wants to conceal the fraud and gets the Legislature to pass a rule that you can't have your penny back. Then the President has his people (the Treasury) sell off the pennies and pockets the cash. Ridiculous, isn't it? But that's exactly what has happened. President Franklin Delano Roosevelt required everyone to turn in their gold for an equivalent face amount of paper and prohibited gold's redemption. The Treasury sold off some of the gold recently, getting 500 to 600 "dollars" per ounce. Recently, I saw a Treasury advertisement offering silver dollars for a minimum "bid" of 150 "dollars." Remember your suitcase you turned in for a piece of paper? They won't redeem your claim check, and now they are selling off the luggage and keeping the cash. Fair? MEGAFRAUD!

My currency is private currency. A hundred years ago, banks, railroads and others circulated private currency. It was Constitutional then. The Constitution has not been amended on this point since, so I claim it is Constitutional now. All paper is redeemable only by the issuer. Since I issued this, it is redeemable only with me.[12] If I do not do what I claim, I would be guilty of fraud. My currency is sold on a "money-back" basis. If you don't like the paper, you can get your money (gold coin) back. The FRN's are passed out on a "nothing-back" basis. If you don't like the paper, you get nothing else. Some might express concern because no one independently "guarantees" my paper. But the government paper, which everyone presumes is good, reflects that over the past 50 years, the government has taken about 98 percent of the value out of it. Isn't that a nice "guarantee?" MEGAFRAUD. My paper is not legal tender. You may not force anyone to take it. It is not money. It is not (yet) widely acceptable. It is not easily divisible. For half a bill you do not get half a $20 coin. As an individual, I could be prosecuted for fraud. But you cannot prosecute the Federal Reserve Board for fraud. Congress can't even audit it. With honest currency you have some control (claim) over the issuer. With dishonest currency you don't even have that.

But you can use honest currency. It might even help you with your taxes. Justice Learned Hand once wrote: "Over and over again courts have said that there is nothing sinister in so arranging one's affairs to keep taxes as low as possible. ...To demand more in the name of morals is mere cant."

How to use it? Ask your boss to pay you in honest currency. The same value would be about 1/50th of the face. If you don't make $3,000, you don't even have to file an income tax return. Since the courts have ruled that there's no difference between an irredeemable note and gold or silver, it doesn't seem as though they could make a distinction between that and a note which **is** equivalent to gold or silver. Or, suppose you were looking for a lawn tractor, with a "price" of $1,000. You ask the merchant, "How much is that in honest money?" After an explanation he might feel $20 was a fair value. Look what happens to this merchant who gets honest currency. He might have costs of perhaps $750 in this tractor. But he sold it for $20. That gives him an accounting "loss" of $730. He could sell three more tractors and hardly have any net income.

Or consider your grandparents who still have the farm they bought 50 years ago. If they give it to you (the heirs), there is a gift tax to pay. If they sell it, there is a capital-gains tax to pay, all because the currency has been destroyed. But suppose they **sold** it to their heirs at a fair value in honest currency. If that were the same price they paid for it when currency was honest, there wouldn't be any capital-gains tax. If the currency were put in a safe-deposit box, then the main asset after death would be cash. But the amount would be so low that it would probably come under the levels excluded from inheritance tax. And besides, the transfer tax on the sale (which is usually a percentage of the sale price) would be a lot lower. You couldn't pay that tax in private currency because it is not legal tender. You could pay the tax in phony money (FRNs) since that is legal tender.

Being based on gold, my private currency does have the characteristic of being a good storage of value. When first issued in 1977, the FRN was 1/236th of mine: now it is approximately 1/1000th of mine. Of course, most people would state it in the reverse: Three years ago, the "price" was $236, now it is $1,000.[13] The statements are equivalent.

My best story about "storage of value" comes from an advertisement a student brought me from a 1901 publication. It offered a new Oldsmobile for $650. The ad stated you could run this car for 10,000 miles in one year for less than $40. If you had saved that $650 as gold coins in a coffee can, that $650 (gold coins) would still buy a new Oldsmobile today and that $40 (gold coins) would still run it for 10,000 miles. However, if you had saved the same **amount** in greenbacks, the $650 (FRNs) would only buy an accessory (air conditioner) for your Olds and the $40 (FRNs) would run it only three weeks (600 miles). That is what I mean by honest money preserving purchasing power.

Also, you might note that the current law with respect to gifts prohibits the giving of more than $3,000 without filing a gift-tax return. That is $3,000 per person, per year. Didn't our forefathers have a right to make gifts without getting a license or paying a tax?

Another thing you might do is ask your Congressman if he believes in complying with his oath to support and defend the Constitution. He has taken that oath, you know. Ask him about requiring States to use gold and silver coin to pay their debts, as the Constitution specifically requires (Article I, Section 10, Paragraph 1—never amended). Ask candidates how they stand on complying with the Constitution. If they are evasive and seem like they will not comply with the Constitution, impeachment is the proper course. But that is too difficult. The best thing is to help them become unemployed after the next election. Find and support an oath-abiding challenger.

In your becoming more informed on this matter, you will have a little additional problem. There are others who will give you specific individual advice. Examples of such advice include buying gold or silver, antiques, postage stamps, etc. You should note that this type of advice helps you cope with the results of inflation and does nothing to correct the cause of it. I have never found an example where you can cure a problem by working on the results of it. You must get to the cause. In this case, if you are personally successful in minimizing the results of inflation, you merely make yourself a bigger target for the government which is the cause of the problem. You become like a plump chicken for the government fox. This is called "loophole closing." For example, in the early days of the income tax, all taxes paid to State and local agencies were excluded. As the government's inflation shoved people into higher brackets, more and more people itemized their returns. So the government attacks itemizing by terminating deductions that were previously allowed. The taxes paid on cigarettes is one example. The taxes paid to license your automobile is another example. The tax paid for a driver's license is another. The transfer tax paid to sell your house is another example. The most recent one is the elimination of the tax paid to the States for gasoline. Millions of people are defrauded into thinking the government owns everything and that you should be grateful for any crumbs of your efforts you are allowed to keep. I say MEGAFRAUD!

Wealth is not necessary to recognize honesty. I am not rich, but I have recognized this problem.[14] I am not the first to recognize this problem, but as far as I know my direct confrontation of the situation is unique.

Some may ask, "Why are you doing this?" Many years ago as a West Point cadet, when I took the oath to defend the Constitution against all enemies, foreign and domestic,

I did not realize the extent of the domestic enemies; I probably still don't. And I must admit to being "tardy" in really studying the Constitution. I sincerely believe that this country has special and unique values which are worth preserving. Many of these values are being silently ground away, and I believe this fraudulent currency scheme is a critical part of the process. My studies indicate the present method of printing fraudulent currency is not Constitutional. In order to have honest dealings between the citizens, it is necessary to have honest currency. This applies also between the citizens and the government.

It's obvious something must be done. But why by ME? Well, if not me, who? The Congress? Members of Congress are the primary source of the present dishonest scheme as well as the chief beneficiaries. They have no real reasons to stop problems. Their jobs depend on the creation of problems. If politicians solved problems, they would be out of jobs. The Federal Administration? They do not make laws. They just carry them out. The court system or Supreme Court? They don't make laws either; they rule on challenges. Big corporate leaders? They can work effectively in the present system. They can be subjected to special pressures if they "rock the boat." Big labor leaders? They, too, are functioning quite well under the present system. Small businessman? It takes little adverse publicity to wipe out a small business. Typical individual? This is the person who will be most helped by an honest money system, but far too few people understand how the present dishonest system works and how they are being defrauded by it. Further, most people have jobs and can be fired all too easily. Me? I don't even have a job; I'm retired. I can't be fired from retirement. My studies have led me to what seems to be a good understanding of the problem. I could be wrong. It could be illegal to have honest currency, but I don't think so.

It takes time for startling truths to be accepted as the realities of life, but though the process of understanding may be slow, it does make sense to the thinking person. Is it any wonder then that the mood of the country has changed from indifference to alarm?

Even the passive people are being aroused. There is the fright of those who awake to startling danger. The words that once lulled them into a sense of security they now find to be utterly false. A new perception exposes the seductive lie.

What of their shattered dreams, their lost hopes and the shreds of their personal ambitions? Where is that something special, that moment of glory that life promised them? The air of pessimism has spread over the land. Who can blame the people? Frightened people, maddened, angry, believing in nothing at all. That is the way it is.

Somebody must get started on a solution. This, I am doing.

CHAPTER V

What Will Solving The Problem Mean?

In many respects I am a tired American. I wish it weren't necessary to stir things up so government's fraudulent actions will be exposed. But it is. Robert Ringer in his book, *Restoring the American Dream,* covers that aspect well. I'm tired of being tricked and forced into buying programs I didn't need and don't want. Besides that, they don't work. It's like going to a fine restaurant, ordering the best meal, paying for it and then getting served sawdust. Perhaps the ultimate insult is being told I should be happy with it since that's the best they can do. MEGAFRAUD!

I could manage without the notoriety that a forthright action brings. With my retirement, a part-time job here and there, some investments and careful planning, I could "make out." That would leave the situation to my children. I understand enough of what is going on to keep my head above water. But should I **have** to be that much of an expert to survive?

Consider a baby boy orphaned by an accident. There is a complete system in place to take care of him. The child can't take care of himself, and that's the way the system should work. What would you think of the system if it sold that boy into slavery? After all, he didn't object, did he? Generally speaking, we are all economic infants. The system should not enslave us. But that's the way it's working now. We are trapped with this fraudulent currency. You earn some extra to replace the "wilt," and you are taxed more. It's like trying to row up a waterfall: You work as hard as you can, straining at the oars, throwing up a spray from your effort, and don't advance a bit.

It is interesting to note that a free nation's currency is a reflection of its strength, and vice versa. The "price" of gold per ounce is really the world's collective opinion of how well we're doing. As in golf, the low score wins. A "score" of $20 is perfect. At least when that was the score, we were the world's leaders, not only in production but freedom and vigor. A score of $35 wasn't too bad; at least we were in the game. But now the score is $700 and has been as high as $875. The daily **change** has been as much as the **total** used to be. Some people think we are likely to hit $1,000, which would be one-fiftieth of our score in better years. Think about it.

Perhaps more striking is that fact that honest currency leads to freedom. It becomes worthwhile to work and save. Dishonest currency leads to slavery; the frustration becomes complete, and the people will accept a tyrant in an attempt to solve their problems. It need not be so. I have two basic guidelines for government (and other) programs:

1. Does it do what it claims?
2. Is it worth what it costs?

Both questions should be answered by the one footing the bill.

My favorite story that distinguishes between things worth doing and things not worth doing concerns a worker at Ft. McHenry who for years had a job polishing the cannon. One day his wife went to get him up as usual and he said, "I don't have to go out to work anymore." She asked why, and he said, "I've retired. I've saved my money and gone into business for myself." "What are you going to do," his wife asked. "Just like always," he said, "I've bought my own cannon. It's in the basement and now I can polish it here."

With honest currency, Congress will be more responsible to the people who create the goods and services that are so wantonly dissipated. The big part of the cost now hidden will be visible. People will see. And the cost is huge.

Consider a little example. Recently, I sharpened some kitchen knives for a friend. In appreciation she baked me a delightful pie. Suppose the value of the pie (in FRNs) was $7 with the cost of ingredients at $5. If $7 were a fair price for my talents, then she obtained them for $5. That's a good deal for her and for me. But if she put her **same skill** into the gross national product (GNP) as a small business, if you assume a typical tax on the extra earnings of 30 percent, then she would have a net profit per pie of $1.40 after taxes. She would have to bake and sell a total of five pies to have $7 left to hire my services. That four extra pies is too high a price to pay. Similarly, if I wanted $7 **cash** to spend I would have to earn $1 to have $7 left after taxes. That would require two **more** pies, for a total of seven. One pie for me and six for "the system." After a while, you decide it's not worth the trouble, and you go fishing. When enough people go fishing, nothing gets done. That's called "recession." An extension of this example indicates why reasonable housing is becoming "just a memory."

Honest currency would change this. With Congress more attentive to getting full value for taxes spent, the taxes would be dramatically smaller. Since it **was** before my time, I don't have first-hand knowledge of how things were when our "world score" was $20, but the total percent of our national effort (GNP) that was spent by government at **all levels** was about 6 percent. Now, it is approaching 50 percent. And as I said before, we are not buying **solutions** with the additional expenditures; we are buying **problems.** Some people can't tell the difference.

With honest currency, work itself becomes worthwhile. As a result, jobs would be more plentiful. All who want would have a job. Each person would have greater incentive to develop his potential since he would keep more out of what he accomplished.

Savings would become real again, and it is from savings that capital is formed. It is from capital that increases in our standard of living come. There has been no net capital formation in our country for 15 years. Attempts to save have proven nearly fruitless. A good example of the pointlessness of saving was in a recent newspaper article. At an auction a person bought a brass bed that hadn't been used for 50 years. Inside the posts was stuffed some cash. The total was nearly $10,000. Of course, the buyer was delighted with his unexpected find. (People who appear to get something for nothing are always delighted.) The interesting thing to me was that in the past 50 years, the government, which didn't even know of the savings, had drained out 98 percent of the value anyway. Congress thinks that's "neat." And they're "fair" —they treat all savings the same way.

Abiding by the Constitution with respect to the currency might encourage Congress to abide by it in other ways. For example, according to Article I, Section 9, Paragraph 7, "No money shall be drawn from the Treasury, but in consequence of appropriations made by law." This means spending "money" it doesn't have is not allowed, but it does it anyway.

These problems are not new. The Constitution anticipated them when it was written. Also, before the turn of the century, during the Democrat Party's convention of 1896, William Jennings Bryan, in a dramatic plea for an increased amount of currency, gave his speech now known as the "Cross of Gold" in which he asked that the nation approve the issuing of currency based not only on gold but also on silver. He was not elected, but the idea of basing currency on silver was accepted, and a ratio of 16:1 was established (that is, 16 parts of silver is equal to one part gold). To that idea of bimetallism William Bourke Cockran responded by saying, "I believe that if he (Bryan) himself understood the inevitable consequences of the doctrines he preaches, his own hands would be the very first to tear down the platform on which he stands." These consequences are now upon us. Certainly, more currency was desired by many of the people. This desire for more currency is normal since most people confuse currency with wealth. The question is not, as William Jennings Bryan so eloquently asked, "Shall we crucify mankind on a Cross of Gold?" But rather, "Shall we accept for ourselves the burden of the "Cross of Honesty?" I say, "Yes, let's be honest." I believe the Constitution also says, "Yes," to this question.

Certainly, we have problems. Maybe that's what life is all about. Certainly, God or the forces of nature will give us sufficient challenges to test our mettle. But I don't see why we should work so hard to create problems we never had and work so hard to make the ones we do have as bad as possible. A thing that is particularly frustrating to me is that problems that are created by government programs are "attacked" with more government programs. That's the description of our "energy crisis."

I recognize that not everyone favors complying with the Constitution. It can be terribly inconvenient. It's like complying with other laws. I could get places a lot faster if I didn't have to worry about stop signs. The Constitution is a series of stop signs for the government. These stop signs are being ignored. The Constitution prohibits rotten money. The stop sign "No Rotten Money" is the key one being ignored, and ignoring it is the source of many of our problems. If people who work for the government (from the President on down) are not in favor of Constitutional compliance, I invite them to stand up and say in a loud, firm voice, "I resign." For each has taken an oath of office which includes being bound by and supporting the Constitution.

It's embarrassing to point out that in the delightful fable by Hans Christian Andersen, The Emperor's Clothes, the Emperor actually is naked. Perhaps you recall the story in which the Emperor orders new clothes but is defrauded by two super con men who tell him they are weaving the finest fabric on their looms, when, in fact, they are making nothing. The peculiar quality of this fantasy fabric is that only those who are truly loyal will see it. Those who are false and disloyal will think nothing is there. When he is finally clothed in this material, the Emperor sees that nothing is there, but believes if he says there is nothing, this will show him as being false. Therefore, he does not admit to seeing nothing. But a child, who observes with unpoliticized eyes, says, "The Emperor is naked!"

In similar fashion, my story giving "indecent exposure" to our national money system has shown you how we have been compromised. It is past time to do something about it. Spread the alarm! Complying with the Constitution is the key.

Abraham Lincoln once said, "All that is necessary for evil to triumph is that good men do nothing." How about you? Get and use honest currency. It will make a difference in your life. With honest savings there is no "guaranteed confiscation" as is now the case.

William Jennings Bryan in that same "Cross of Gold" speech said, "The humblest citizen in all the land, when clad in the armor of a righteous cause, is stronger than all the hosts of error." Victor Hugo wrote, "Nothing else in the world, not all the armies, is so powerful as an idea whose time has come."

Perhaps this is an idea whose time has come.

References

[1]MONOPOLY® is the Parker Brother's registered trademark for its real estate trading game equipment. Used by permission.

[2]FRAUD: An intentional twisting of truth for the purpose of tricking another, depending upon it, to part with some valuable thing belonging to him or to surrender a legal right.

[3]In 2011, the total debt is more than $14 trillion and equals more than $233,000 per person or almost $1 million per family of four.

[4]*A Time for Truth*, William E. Simon, Berkley Books. 1979. Used with the permission of McGraw-Hill Book Company.

[5]World Research INK, Summer 1980.

[6]*Wall Street Journal*, June 24, 1980.

[7]The American Revolution, C.H. McIlwain, p. 151.

[8]RIGHT: That which is due anyone by legal and/or moral principles.

[9]Darland discontinued this offer, and it is no longer valid.

[10]Darland discontinued this offer after a few years. This is no longer a valid offer, and it will not be revived.

[11]**"Right"** is distinct from a **privilege.** A privilege is not available to all. If you must have a license for an activity, it is a privilege. If anyone may do it and you need no license, it is a **right.**

[12]Since I am mortal, the currency has an expiration date. If I should die before then, provisions have been made for redemption of all currency outstanding.

[13]The "double eagle" is one Troy ounce of gold, 9/10ths fine (464.4 grams pure gold), but the price is higher than one Troy ounce (480 grams) of pure gold because of the numismatic (collector) value. The typical premium is 25 percent to 45 percent.

[14]**NOTE:** Obviously, the gold backing would not be kept in a residence but under professional security. Because of the uniqueness of this approach, I have consulted professionals about personal security.

Index

gold standard 33

Goldwater, Barry, Senator 43

Greek 51

greenbacks 61

gross national product (GNP) 67

growth 31, 41, 52

H

Hale vs. Henkel 58

hard money 21

Harford Community College 14

Harford County Gifted and Talented Association 14

honest currency 22, 43, 50, 59, 60, 63, 64, 66, 67, 68, 70

honest money system 16, 17, 63

Hugo, Victor 71

I

Imperial Rome 15

income tax 15, 18, 19, 28, 33, 42, 53, 56, 57, 58, 60, 62

indirect taxes 57

inflating 19

inflation 7, 8, 9, 15, 16, 20, 23, 24, 25, 26, 27, 31, 32, 34, 39, 40, 42, 56, 62

inheritance tax 60

International Monetary Fund (IMF) 42

IRS 10, 42, 58

J

Jefferson, Thomas, President 32

judicial 51

Justice Learned Hand 59

K

King George 47

Keynes, John Maynard 12

L

Latin 51

lawful money 22

legal 12, 57, 72

legal tender 25, 59, 60

legislative 51

legislature 17, 19, 58

liability 26

Lincoln, Abraham 70

loophole 31,

loophole closing 62

Notes:

Notes:

Notes: